T0107203

The Mastery *of* Destiny

JAMES ALLEN TITLES

———◦◆◦———

Above Life's Turmoil

All These Things Added

As a Man Thinketh

Byways of Blessedness

Eight Pillars of Prosperity

Foundation Stones to Happiness and Success

From Passion to Peace

From Poverty to Power

James Allen's Book of Meditations for Every Day in the Year

Light on Life's Difficulties

Man: King of Mind, Body, and Circumstance

Men and Systems

Morning and Evening Thoughts

Out from the Heart

Poems of Peace

The Life Triumphant

The Mastery of Destiny

The Shining Gateway

Through the Gate of Good

The Mastery of Destiny

James Allen

MEDIA

Published 2019 by Gildan Media LLC
aka G&D Media
www.GandDmedia.com

No part of this book may be used, reproduced or transmitted in any manner whatsoever, by any means (electronic, photocopying, recording, or otherwise), without the prior written permission of the author, except in the case of brief quotations embodied in critical articles and reviews. No liability is assumed with respect to the use of the information contained within. Although every precaution has been taken, the author and publisher assume no liability for errors or omissions. Neither is any liability assumed for damages resulting from the use of the information contained herein.

Design by Meghan Day Healey of Story Horse, LLC

Library of Congress Cataloging-in-Publication Data is available upon request

ISBN: 978-1-7225-0244-7

10   9   8   7   6   5   4   3   2   1

Contents

Preface

The discovery of the law of Evolution in the material world has prepared men for a knowledge of the law of cause and effect in the mental world. Thought is not less orderly and progressive than the material forms which embody thought; and not alone cells and atoms, but thoughts and deeds are charged with a cumulative and selective energy. In the realm of thought and deed, the *good* survives, for it is "fittest"; the *evil* ultimately perishes. To know that the "perfect law" of Causation is as all-embracing in mind as in matter, is to be relieved from all anxiety concerning the ultimate destiny of individuals and of humanity—

For man is man and master of his fate—

and the will in man which is conquering the knowledge of natural law will conquer the knowledge of spiritual law; the will which, in ignorance, chooses evil, will, as wisdom evolves and emerges, choose good. In a universe of law, the final mastery of evil by man is assured. His lesser destinies of separation and sorrow, defeat and death, are but disciplinary steps leading to the Great Destiny of triumphal mastery. He himself is unconsciously building, albeit with lacerated hands and labour-bowed form, the Temple of Glory which is to afford him an eternal habitation of peace.

In this volume I have tried to set down some words indicative of this Law and this Destiny, and the manner of its working and its building; and have so arranged the subject-matter as to make the book a companion volume to *The Life Triumphant*. The first six, and the last, chapters first appeared in *Bibby's Quarterly* and *Bibby's Annual*, and it is by kind permission of the Editor, Mr. Joseph Bibby, that they are now brought together and published in volume form, the other three chapters having been added to make the book consecutive and complete.

—James Allen
*Bryngoleu,
Ilfracombe, England
April, 1909*

Deeds, Character, and Destiny

There is, and always has been, a wide-spread belief in Fate, or Destiny; that is, in an eternal and inscrutable Power which apportions definite ends to both individuals and nations. This belief has arisen from long observation of the facts of life. Men are conscious that there are certain occurrences which they cannot control, and are powerless to avert. Birth and death, for instance, are inevitable, and many of the incidents of life appear equally inevitable. Men strain every nerve for the attainment of certain ends, and gradually they become conscious of a Power which seems to be not of themselves, which frustrates their puny efforts, and laughs, as it were, at their fruitless striving and struggle. As men advance in life, they learn to submit, more or less, to this overruling Power which they do not understand, perceiving only its effects in themselves and the world around them, and they call it by various names, such as God, Providence, Fate, Destiny, etc.

Men of contemplation, such as poets and philosophers, step aside, as it were, to watch the movements of this mysterious Power as it seems to elevate its favourites on the one hand, and strike down its victims on the other, without reference to merit or demerit. The greatest poets, especially the dramatic poets, represent this Power in their works, as they have observed it in Nature. The Greek and Roman dramatists usually depict their heroes as having foreknowledge of their fate, and taking means to escape it; but by so doing they blindly involve themselves in a series of consequences which bring about the doom which they are trying to avert. Shakespeare's characters, on the other hand, are represented, as in Nature, with no foreknowledge (except in the form of presentiment) of their particular destiny. Thus, according to the poets, whether the man knows his fate or not, he cannot avert it, and every conscious or unconscious act of his is a step toward it.

Omar Khayyam's "Moving Finger" is a vivid expression of this idea of Fate:

The Moving Finger writes, and having writ,
Moves on: nor all thy Piety nor Wit
Shall lure it back to cancel half a line,
Nor all thy Tears wash out a Word of it.

Thus, men in all nations and times have experienced in their lives the action of this invincible Power or Law, and in our nation today this experience has been crystallized in the terse proverb, "Man proposes, God disposes."

But, contradictory as it may appear, there is an equally wide-spread belief in man's responsibility as a free agent.

All moral teaching is an affirmation of man's freedom to choose his course and mould his destiny; and man's patient and untiring efforts in achieving his ends are declarations of consciousness of freedom and power. This dual experience of fate on the one hand, and freedom on the other, has given rise to the interminable controversy between the believers in Fatalism and the upholders of Free-will—a controversy which was recently revived under the term "Determinism *versus* Free-will." Between apparently conflicting extremes there is always a "middle way" of balance, justice, or compensation which, while it includes both extremes, cannot be said to be either one or the other, and which brings both into harmony; and this middle way is the point of contact between two extremes. Truth cannot be a partisan, but, by its nature, is the Reconciler of extremes; and so, in the matter which we are considering, there is a "golden mean" which brings Fate and Free-will into close relationship, wherein, indeed, it is seen that these two indisputable facts in human life, for such they are, are but two aspects of one central law, one unifying and all-embracing principle, namely, *the law of causation in its moral aspect.*

Moral causation necessitates both Fate and Free-will, both individual responsibility and individual predestination, for the law of causes must also be the law of effects, and cause and effect must always be equal; the train of causation, both in matter and mind, must be eternally balanced, therefore eternally just, eternally perfect. Thus every effect may be said to be a thing *preordained*, but the pre-determining power is a cause, and not the fiat of an arbitrary will.

Man finds himself involved in the train of causation. His life is made up of causes and effects. It is both a sowing and a reaping. Each act of his is a cause which must be balanced by its effects. He chooses the cause (this is Free-will), he cannot choose, alter, or avert the effect (this is Fate); thus Free-will stands for the power to initiate causes, and destiny is involvement in effects. It is therefore true that man is predestined to certain ends, but he himself has (though he knows it not) issued the mandate; that good or evil thing from which there is no escape, he has, by his own deeds, brought about.

It may here be urged that man is not responsible for his deeds, that these are the effects of his character, and that he is not responsible for the character, good or bad, which was given him at his birth. If character was "given him" at birth, this would be true, and there would then be no moral law, and no need for moral teaching; but characters are not given ready-made, they are *evolved*; they are, indeed, effects, the products of the moral law itself, that is—the products of deeds. Character is the combined result of an incalculable number of deeds, is, in reality, an accumulation of deeds which has been piled up, so to speak, by the individual during vast ages of time and through innumerable lives, by a slow process of orderly evolution. A man's birth into this life, with his complex character, to which he considers himself irresponsibly predestined, was determined by his own deeds in former lives.

Man is the doer of his own deeds; as such he is the maker of his own character; and as the doer of his deeds and the maker of his character, he is the moulder and shaper of his destiny. He has the power to modify and alter his deeds, and every time he acts he modifies his character, and with the modification of his character for good or evil, he is predetermining for himself new destinies—destinies disastrous or beneficent in accordance with the nature of his deeds. Character is destiny itself; as a fixed combination of deeds, it bears within itself the results of those deeds. These results lie hidden as moral seeds in the dark recesses of the character, awaiting their season of germination, growth, and fruitage.

Those things which befall a man are the reflections of himself; that destiny which pursued him, which he was powerless to escape by effort, or avert by prayer, was the relentless ghoul of his own wrong deeds demanding and enforcing restitution; those blessings and curses which come to him unbidden are the reverberating echoes of the sounds which he himself sent forth.

It is this knowledge of the Perfect Law working through and above all things; of the Perfect Justice operating in and adjusting all human affairs, that enables the good man to love his enemies, and to rise above all hatred, resentment, and complaining; for he knows that only his own can come to him, and that, though he be surrounded by persecutors, his enemies are but the blind instruments of a faultless retribution; and so he blames them not, but calmly receives his accounts, and patiently pays his moral debts.

But this is not all; he does not merely pay his debts; he takes care not to contract any further debts. He watches himself and makes his deeds faultless. While paying off evil accounts, he is laying up good accounts. By putting an end to his own sin, he is bringing evil and suffering to an end.

And now let us consider how the Law operates in particular instances in the outworking of destiny through deeds and character. First, we will look at this present life, for the present is the synthesis of the entire past; the net result of all that a man has ever thought and done is contained within him. It is noticeable that sometimes the good man fails and the unscrupulous man prospers—a fact which seems to put all moral maxims as to the good results of righteousness out of account—and because of this, many people deny the operation of any just law in human life, and even declare that it is chiefly the unjust that prosper. Nevertheless, the moral law exists, and is not altered or subverted by shallow conclusions. It should be remembered that man is *a changing, evolving being.* The good man was not always good; the bad man was not always bad. Even in this life (without, for the moment, going back to former lives), there was a time, in a large number of instances, when the man who is now just, was unjust; when he who is now kind, was cruel; when he who is now pure, was impure. Obversely, there was a time in this life, in a number of instances, when he who is now unjust, was just; when he who is now cruel, was kind; when he who is now impure, was pure. Thus, the good man who is overtaken with calamity today is reaping the result of his former evil sowing; later he will reap the happy result of his present good sowing; while the bad man is now reaping the result of his former good sowing; later he will reap the result of his present sowing of bad. But when just causes (of the effects which we see) are not apparent in this life, then they were set going in former lives; and, indeed, the entire evolution of any being, through innumerable births and deaths and ever-enlarging destinies, may be regarded as one long, extended, unbroken line of causes and effects; one indestructible, ever-growing, ever-changing, and ascending life.

Characteristics are fixed habits of mind, the results of deeds. An act repeated a large number of times becomes unconscious, or automatic—that is, it then seems to repeat itself without any effort on the part of the doer, so that it seems to him almost impossible not to do it, and then it has become a mental characteristic. Thus, the character of an individual at birth is a combination of habits which he himself has built up by his own thoughts and acts during the course of his evolution, and in accordance with his efforts in this life will his character be modified for good or evil in the future.

Here is a poor man out of work. He is honest, and is not a shirker. He wants work, and cannot get it. He tries hard, and continues to fail. Where is the justice in his lot? There was a time in this man's condition when he had plenty of work. He felt burdened with it; he shirked it, and longed for ease. He thought how delightful it would be to have nothing to do. He did not appreciate the blessedness of his lot. His desire for ease is now gratified, but the fruit for which he longed, and which he thought would taste so sweet, has turned to ashes in his mouth. The condition which he aimed for, namely, to have nothing to do, he has reached, and there he is compelled to remain till his lesson is thoroughly learned. And he is surely learning that habitual ease is degrading, that to have nothing to do is a condition of wretchedness, and that work is a noble and blessed thing. His former desires and deeds have brought him where he is; and now his present desire for work, his ceaseless searching and asking for it, will just as surely bring about

its own beneficent result. No longer desiring idleness, his present condition will, as an effect, the
cause of which is no longer propagated, soon pass
away, and he will obtain employment; and if his
whole mind is now set on work, and he desires it
above all else, then when it comes he will be over-
whelmed with it; it will flow in to him from all
sides, and he will prosper in his industry. Then, if
he does not understand the law of cause and effect
in human life, he will wonder why work comes to
him apparently unsought, while others who seek it
strenuously fail to obtain it.

Nothing comes unbidden; where the shadow
is, there also is the substance. That which comes
to the individual is the product of his own deeds.
As cheerful industry leads to greater industry
and increasing prosperity, and labour shirked or
undertaken discontentedly leads to a lesser degree
of labour and decreasing prosperity, so with all
the varied conditions of life as we see them—they
are *the effects of deeds*, destinies wrought by the
thoughts and deeds of each particular individual.
So also with the vast variety of characters—they
are the ripening and ripened growth of the sowing
of deeds, a sowing not Confined solely to this visible life, but going backward through that Infinite
life which traverses the portals of innumerable
births and deaths, and which also will extend into

the illimitable future, reaping its own harvests, eating the sweet and bitter fruits of its own deeds.

It is thus literally true that when men die they "go to heaven or hell," in accordance with their deeds. But the heaven and hell are in this world. The rich man who abused his wealth or who obtained his riches by fraud or oppression, is reborn in poverty and shame. The poor man who used the little he possessed wisely and unselfishly is reborn in plenty and honour. The cruel and unjust are reborn in the midst of harsh and untoward surroundings; the kind and just are reborn where kind hearts and gentle hands watch over and tend them. Thus, with every vice and virtue, each receives its own; each declares its own destiny.

But even those who refuse to believe in rebirth will find that even in this life men almost invariably reap what they sow; and the time is surely coming when social and political reformers will pay more attention to the development of character than the mere gaining of party issues. As the individual reaps what he sows, so the nation, being a community of individuals, reaps also what it sows. Nations become great when their leaders are just men; they fall and fade when their just men pass away. Those who are in power set an example, good or bad, for the entire nation. Great will be the peace and prosperity of a nation when there shall arise within it a line of statesmen who, having first established themselves in a lofty integrity of character, shall direct the energies of the nation toward the culture of virtue and development of character, knowing that only through personal industry, integrity, and nobility can national prosperity proceed.

Still, above all, is the Great Law, calmly and with infallible justice meting out to mortals their fleeting destinies, tear-stained or smiling, the fabric of their hands. Life is a great school for the development of character, and all, through strife and struggle, vice and virtue, success and failure, are slowly but surely learning the lessons of wisdom.

The Science of
Self-Control

We live in a scientific age. Men of science are numbered by thousands, and they are ceaselessly searching, analyzing, and experimenting with a view to discovery and the increase of knowledge. The shelves of our libraries, both public and private, are heavy with their load of imposing volumes on scientific subjects, and the wonderful achievements of modern science are always before us—whether in our homes or in our streets, in country or town, on land or sea—there shall we have before us some marvellous device, some recent accomplishment of science, for adding to our comfort, increasing our so speed, or saving the labour of our hands.

Yet, with all our vast store of scientific knowledge, and its startling and rapidly increasing results in the world of discovery and invention, there is, in this age, one branch of science which has so far fallen into decay as to have become almost forgotten; a science, nevertheless, which is of greater importance than all the other sciences combined, and without which all science would but subserve the ends of selfishness, and aid in man's destruction—I refer to the *Science of Self-control.*

Our modern scientists study the elements and forces which are outside themselves, with the object of controlling and utilizing them. The ancients studied the elements and forces which were within themselves, with a view to controlling and utilizing them, and the ancients produced such mighty Masters of knowledge in this direction, that to this day they are held in reverence as gods, and the vast religious organizations of the world are based upon their achievements.

Wonderful as are the forces in nature, they are vastly inferior to that combination of intelligent forces which comprise the mind of man, and which dominate and direct the blind mechanical forces of nature. Therefore, it follows that, to understand, control, and direct the inner forces of passion, desire, will, and intellect, is to be in possession of the destinies of men and nations.

As in ordinary science, there are, in this divine science, degrees of attainment; and a man is great in knowledge, great in himself, and great in his influence on the world, in the measure that he is great in self-control.

He who understands and dominates the forces of external nature is the natural scientist; but he who understands and dominates the internal forces of the mind is the divine scientist; and the laws which operate in gaining a knowledge of external appearances, operate also in gaining a knowledge of internal verities.

A man cannot become an accomplished scientist in a few weeks or months, nay, not even in a few years. But only after many years of painstaking investigation can he speak with authority, and be ranked among the masters of science. Likewise, a man cannot acquire self-control, and become possessed of the wisdom and peace-giving knowledge which that self-control confers, but by many years of patient labour; a labour which is all the more arduous because it is silent, and both unrecognized and unappreciated by others; and he who would pursue this science successfully must learn to stand alone, and to toil unrewarded, as far as any outward emolument is concerned.

The natural scientist pursues, in acquiring his particular kind of knowledge, the following five orderly and sequential steps:

1. **Observation.** That is, he closely and persistently observes the facts of nature.

2. **Experiment.** Having become acquainted, by repeated observations, with certain facts, he experiments with those facts, with a view to the discovery of natural laws. He puts his facts through rigid processes of analysis, and so finds out what is useless and what of value; and he rejects the former and retains the latter.

3. **Classification.** Having accumulated and verified a mass of facts by numberless observations and experiments, he commences to classify those facts, to arrange them in orderly groups with the object of discovering some underlying law, some hidden and unifying principle, which governs, regulates, and binds together these facts.

4. **Deduction.** Thus he passes on to the fourth step of deduction. From the facts and results which are before him, he discovers certain invariable modes of action, and thus reveals the hidden laws of things.

5. **Knowledge.** Having proven and established certain laws, it may be said of such a man that he *knows*. He is a scientist, a man of knowledge.

But the attainment of scientific knowledge is not the end, great as it is. Men do not attain knowledge for themselves alone, nor to keep it locked secretly in their hearts, like a beautiful jewel in a dark chest. The end of such knowledge is use, service, the increase of the comfort and happiness of the world. Thus, when a man has become a scientist, he gives the world the benefit of his knowledge, and unselfishly bestows upon mankind the results of all his labours. Thus, beyond knowledge, there is a further step of *Use*: that is, the right and unselfish use of the knowledge acquired; the application of knowledge to invention for the common weal.

It will be noted that the five steps or processes enumerated follow in orderly succession, and that no man can become a scientist who omits any one of them. Without the first step of systematic observation, for instance, he could not even enter the realm of knowledge of nature's secrets. At first, the searcher for such knowledge has before him a universe of *things*: these things he does not understand; many of them, indeed, seem to be irreconcilably opposed one to the other, and there is apparent confusion; but by patiently and laboriously pursuing these five processes, he discovers the order, nature, and essences of things; perceives the central law or laws which bind them together in harmonious relationship, and so puts an end to confusion and ignorance.

As with the natural scientist, so with the divine scientist; he must pursue, with the same self-sacrificing diligence, five progressive steps in the attainment of self-knowledge, self-control. These five steps are the same as with the natural scientist, but *the process is reversed*, the mind, instead of being centred upon external things, is turned back upon itself, and the investigations are pursued in the realm of mind (of one's own mind) instead of in that of matter. At first, the searcher for divine knowledge is confronted with that mass of desires, passions, emotions, ideas, and intellections which he calls himself, which is the basis of all his actions, and from which his life proceeds.

This combination of invisible, yet powerful, forces appears confusedly; some of them stand, apparently, in direct conflict with each other, without any appearance or hope of reconciliation; his mind in its entirety, too, with his life which proceeds from that mind, does not seem to have any equitable relation to many other minds and lives about him, and altogether there is a condition of pain and confusion from which he would fain escape. Thus, he begins by keenly realizing his state of ignorance, for no one could acquire either natural or divine knowledge, if he were convinced that without study or labour he already possessed it. With such perception of one's ignorance, there comes the desire for knowledge, and the novice in self-control enters upon the ascending pathway, in which are the following five steps:

1. **Introspection.** This coincides with the *observation* of the natural scientist. The mental eye is turned like a searchlight upon the inner things of the mind, and its subtle and ever-varying processes are observed and carefully noted. This stepping aside from selfish gratifications, from the excitements of worldly pleasures and ambitions, in order to observe, with the object of understanding, one's nature, is the beginning of self-

control. Hitherto, the man has been blindly and impotently borne along by the impulses of his nature, the mere creature of things and circumstances, but now he puts a check upon his impulses and, instead of being controlled, begins to control.

2. **Self-analysis.** Having observed the tendencies of the mind, they are then closely examined, and are put through a rigid process of analysis. The evil tendencies (those that produce painful effects) are separated from the good tendencies (those that produce peaceful effects); and the various tendencies, with the particular actions they produce, and the definite results which invariably spring from these actions, are gradually grasped by the understanding, which is at last enabled to follow them in their swift and subtle interplay and profound ramifications. It is a process of *testing and proving,* and, for the searcher, a period of being tested and proved.

3. **Adjustment.** By this time, the practical student of things divine has clearly before him every tendency and aspect of his nature, down to the profoundest promptings of his mind, and the most subtle motives of

his heart. There is not a spot or corner left, which he has not explored and illuminated with the light of self-examination. He is familiar with every weak and selfish point, every strong and virtuous quality. It is considered the height of wisdom to be able to see ourselves as others see us, but the practiser of self-control goes far beyond this: he not only sees himself as others see him, he *sees himself as he is*. Thus, standing face to face with himself, not striving to hide away from any secret fault; no longer defending himself with pleasant flatteries; neither underrating nor overrating himself or his powers, and no more cursed with self-praise or self-pity, he sees the full magnitude of the task which lies before him; sees clearly ahead the heights of self-control, and knows what work he has to do to reach them. He is no longer in a state of confusion, but has gained a glimpse of the laws which operate in the world of thought, and he now begins to *adjust* his mind in accordance with those laws. This is a process of *weeding, sifting, cleansing*. As the farmer weeds, cleans, and prepares the ground for his crops, so the student removes the weeds of evil from his mind, cleanses and purifies it preparatory to sowing the seeds of righteous actions which shall produce the harvest of a well-ordered life.

4. **Righteousness.** Having adjusted his thoughts and deeds to those minor laws which operate in mental activities in the production of pain and pleasure, unrest and peace, sorrow and bliss, he now perceives that there is involved in those laws one Great Central Law which, like the law of gravitation in the natural world, is supreme in the world of mind; a law to which all thoughts and deeds are subservient, and by which they are regulated and kept in their proper sphere. This is the law of Justice or Righteousness, which is universal and supreme. To this law he now conforms. Instead of thinking and acting blindly, as the nature is stimulated and appealed to by outward things, he subordinates his thoughts and deeds to this central principle. He no longer acts from self, *but does what is right*—what is universally and eternally right. He is no longer the abject slave of his nature and circumstances, he is the master of his nature and circumstances. He is no longer carried hither and thither on the forces of his mind; he controls and guides those forces to the

accomplishment of his purposes. Thus, having his nature in control and subjection, not thinking thoughts nor doing deeds which oppose the righteous law, and which, therefore, that law annuls with suffering and defeat, he rises above the dominion of sin and sorrow, ignorance and doubt, and is strong, calm, and peaceful.

5. **Pure Knowledge.** By thinking right and acting right, he proves, by experience, the existence of the divine law on which the mind is framed, and which is the guiding and unifying principle in all human affairs and events, whether individual or national. Thus, by perfecting himself in self-control, he acquires divine knowledge; he reaches the point where it may be said of him, as of the natural scientist, that he *knows*. He has mastered the science of self-control, and has brought knowledge out of ignorance, order out of confusion. He has acquired that knowledge of self which includes knowledge of all men; that knowledge of one's own life which embraces knowledge of all lives—for all minds are the same in essence (differing only in degree), are framed upon the same law; and the same thoughts and acts,

by whatsoever individual they are wrought, will always produce the same results.

But this divine and peace-bestowing knowledge, as in the case of the natural scientist, is not gained for one's self alone; for if this were so, the aim of evolution would be frustrated, and it is not in the nature of things to fall short of ripening and accomplishment; and, indeed, he who thought to gain this knowledge solely for his own happiness would most surely fail. So, beyond the fifth step of Pure Knowledge, there is a still further one of *Wisdom*, which is the right application of the knowledge acquired; the pouring out upon the world, unselfishly and without stint, the result of one's labours, thus accelerating progress and uplifting humanity.

It may be said of men who have not gone back into their own nature to control and purify it, that they cannot clearly distinguish between good and evil, right and wrong. They reach after those things which they think will give them pleasure, and try to avoid those things which they believe will cause them pain. The source of their actions is self, and they only discover right painfully and in a fragmentary way, by periodically passing through severe sufferings, and lashings of conscience. But he who practises self-control, passing through the five processes, which are five stages of growth, gains that knowledge which enables him to act from the moral law which sustains the universe. He knows good and evil, right and wrong, and, thus knowing them, lives in accordance with good and right. He no longer needs to consider what is pleasant or what is unpleasant, but does what is right; his nature is in harmony with his conscience, and there is no remorse; his mind is in unison with the Great Law, and there is no more suffering and sin; for him evil is ended, and good is all in all.

Cause and
Effect in Human
Conduct

I t is an axiom with the scientists that every effect
is related to a cause. Apply this to the realm of
human conduct, and there is revealed the principle of *justice*.

Every scientist knows (and now all men believe)
that perfect harmony prevails throughout every
portion of the physical universe, from the speck of
dust to the greatest sun. Everywhere there is exqui-
site adjustment. In the sidereal universe, with its
millions of suns rolling majestically through space
and carrying with them their respective systems
of revolving planets, its vast nebulæ, its seas of

meteors, and its vast army of comets travelling through illimitable space with inconceivable velocity, perfect order prevails; and again, in the natural world, with its multitudinous aspects of life, and its Infinite variety of forms, there are the clearly defined limits of specific laws, through the operation of which all confusion is avoided, and unity and harmony eternally obtain. If this universal harmony could be arbitrarily broken, even in one small particular, the universe would cease to be; there could be no cosmos, but only universal chaos. Nor can it be possible in such a universe of law that there should exist any personal power which is above, outside, and superior to, such law in the sense that it can defy it, or set it aside; for whatsoever beings exist, whether they be men or gods, they exist by virtue of such law; and the highest, best, and wisest among all beings would manifest his greater wisdom by his more complete obedience to that law which is wiser than wisdom, and than which nothing more perfect could be devised.

All things, whether visible or invisible, are subservient to, and fall within the scope of, this infinite and eternal law of *causation*. As all things seen obey it, so all things unseen—the thoughts and deeds of men, whether secret or open—cannot escape it

Do right, it recompenseth; do one wrong,
The equal retribution must be made.

Perfect justice upholds the universe; perfect justice regulates human life and conduct. All the varying conditions of life, as they obtain in the world today, are the result of this law reacting on human conduct. Man can (and does) choose what causes he shall set in operation, but he cannot change the nature of effects; he can decide what thoughts he shall think, and what deeds he shall do, but he has no power over the *results* of those thoughts and deeds; these are regulated by the overruling law.

Man has all power to act, but his power ends with the act committed. The result of the act cannot be altered, annulled, or escaped; it is irrevocable. Evil thoughts and deeds produce conditions of suffering; good thoughts and deeds determine conditions of blessedness. Thus man's power is limited to, and his blessedness or misery is determined by, *his own conduct.* To know this truth, renders life simple, plain, and unmistakable; all the crooked paths are straightened out, the heights of wisdom are revealed, and the open door to salvation from evil and suffering is perceived and entered.

Life may be likened to a sum in arithmetic. It is bewilderingly difficult and complex to the pupil who has not yet grasped the key to its correct solution, but once this is perceived and laid hold of, it becomes as astonishingly simple as it was formerly profoundly perplexing. Some idea of this relative simplicity and complexity of life may be grasped by fully recognizing and realizing the fact that, while there are scores, and perhaps hundreds, of ways in which a sum may be done wrong, *there is only one way by which it can be done right,* and that when that right way is found the pupil *knows it to be the right*; his perplexity vanishes, and he knows that he has mastered the problem.

It is true that the pupil, while doing his sum incorrectly, may (and frequently does) *think* he has done it correctly, but he is not sure; his perplexity is still there, and if he is an earnest and apt pupil, he will recognize his own error when it is pointed out by the teacher. So in life, men may think they are living rightly while they are continuing, through ignorance, to live wrongly; but the presence of doubt, perplexity, and unhappiness are sure indications that the right way has not yet been found.

There are foolish and careless pupils who would like to pass a sum as correct before they have acquired a true knowledge of figures, but the eye and skill of the teacher quickly detect and expose the fallacy. So in life there can be no falsifying of results; the eye of the Great Law reveals and exposes. Twice five will make ten to all eternity, and no amount of ignorance, stupidity, or delusion can bring the result up to eleven.

If one looks superficially at a piece of cloth, he sees it as a piece of cloth, but if he goes further and inquires into its manufacture, and examines it closely and attentively, he sees that it is composed of a combination of individual threads, and that, while all the threads are interdependent, each thread pursues its own way throughout, never becoming confused with its sister thread. It is this entire absence of confusion between the particular threads which constitutes the finished work *a piece of cloth*; any inharmonious commingling of the thread would result in a bundle of *waste* or a useless *rag*.

Life is like a piece of cloth, and the threads of which it is composed are individual lives. The threads, while being interdependent, are not confounded one with the other. Each follows its own course. Each individual suffers and enjoys the consequences of his own deeds, and not of the deeds of another. The course of each is simple and definite; the whole forming a complicated, yet harmonious, combination of sequences. There are action and reaction, deed and consequence, cause and effect, and the counterbalancing reaction, consequence, and effect is always in exact ratio with the initiatory impulse.

A durable and satisfactory piece of cloth cannot be made from shoddy material, and the threads of selfish thoughts and bad deeds will not produce a useful and beautiful life—a life that will wear well, and bear close inspection. Each man makes or mars his own life; it is not made or marred by his neighbour, or by anything external to himself. Each thought he thinks, each deed he does, is another thread—shoddy or genuine—woven into the garment of his life; and as he makes the garment so must he wear it. He is not responsible for his neighbour's deeds; he is not the custodian of his neighbour's actions; he is responsible only for his own deeds; he is the custodian of his own actions.

The "problem of evil" subsists in a man's own evil deeds, and it is solved when those deeds are purified. Says Rosseau:

> Man, seek no longer the origin of evil; thou thyself
>   art its origin.

Effect can never be divorced from cause; it can never be of a different nature from cause. Emerson says:

> Justice is not postponed; a perfect equity adjusts
>   the balance in all parts of life.

And there is a profound sense in which cause and effect are simultaneous, and form one perfect whole. Thus, upon the instant that a man thinks, say, a cruel thought, or does a cruel deed, that same instant be has *injured his own mind*; he is not the same man he was the previous instant; he is a little viler and a little more unhappy; and a number of such successive thoughts and deeds would produce a cruel and wretched man. The same thing applies to the contrary—the thinking of a kind thought, or doing a kind deed—an immediate nobility and happiness attend it; the man is better than he was before, and a number of such deeds would produce a great and blissful soul.

Thus individual human conduct determines, by the faultless law of cause and effect, individual merit or demerit, individual greatness or mean-ness, individual happiness or wretchedness. What a man thinks, that he does; what he does, that he is. If he is perplexed, unhappy, restless, or wretched, let him look to himself, for there and nowhere else is the source of all his trouble.

Training
of the Will

Without strength of mind, nothing worthy of accomplishment can be done, and the cultivation of that steadfastness and stability of character which is commonly called " will-power" is one of the foremost duties of man, for its possession is essentially necessary both to his temporal and eternal well-being. Fixedness of purpose is at the root of all successful efforts, whether in things worldly or spiritual, and without it man cannot be otherwise than wretched, and dependent upon others for that support which should be found within himself.

The mystery which has been thrown around the subject of cultivation of the will by those who advertise to sell "occult advice" on the matter for so many dollars, should be avoided and dispelled, for nothing could be further removed from secrecy and mystery than the practical methods by which alone strength of will can be developed.

The true path of will-cultivation is only to be found in the common everyday life of the individual, and so obvious and simple is it that the majority, looking for something complicated and mysterious, pass it by unnoticed.

A little logical thought will soon convince a man that he cannot be both weak and strong at the same time, that he cannot develop a stronger will while remaining a slave to weak indulgences, and that, therefore, the direct and only way to that greater strength is to assail and conquer his weaknesses. All the means for the cultivation of the will are already at hand in the mind and life of the individual; they reside in the weak side of his character, by attacking and vanquishing which the necessary strength of will will be developed. He who has succeeded in grasping this simple, preliminary truth, will perceive that the whole science of will-cultivation is embodied in the following seven rules:

1. Break off bad habits.
2. Form good habits.

3. Give scrupulous attention to the duty of the present moment.
4. Do vigorously, and at once, whatever has to be done.
5. Live by rule.
6. Control the tongue.
7. Control the mind.

Anyone who earnestly meditates upon, and diligently practises, the above rules, will not fail to develop that purity of purpose and power of will which will enable him to successfully cope with every difficulty, and pass triumphantly through every emergency.

It will be seen that the first step is the breaking away from bad habits. This is no easy task. It demands the putting forth of great efforts, or a succession of efforts, and it is by such efforts that the will can alone be invigorated and fortified. If one refuses to take the first step, he cannot increase in will-power, for by submitting to a bad habit, because of the immediate pleasure which it affords, one forfeits the right to rule over himself, and is so far a weak slave. He who thus avoids self-discipline, and looks about for some "occult secrets" for gaining will-power at the expenditure of little or no effort on his part, is deluding himself, and is weakening the will-power which he already possesses.

The increased strength of will which is gained by success in overcoming bad habits enables one to initiate good habits; for, while the conquering of a bad habit requires merely strength of purpose, the forming of a new one necessitates the *intelligent direction of purpose*. To do this, a man must be mentally active and energetic, and must keep a constant watch upon himself. As a man succeeds in perfecting himself in the second rule, it will not be very difficult for him to observe the third, that of giving scrupulous attention to the duty of the present moment. Thoroughness is a step in the development of the will which cannot be passed over. Slipshod work is an indication of weakness. Perfection should be aimed at, even in the smallest task. By not dividing the mind, but giving the whole attention to each separate task as it presents itself, singleness of purpose and intense concentration of mind are gradually gained—two mental powers which give weight and worth of character, and bring repose and joy to their possessor.

The fourth rule—that of doing vigorously, and at once, whatever has to be done—is equally important. Idleness and a strong will cannot go together, and procrastination is a total barrier to the acquisition of purposeful action. Nothing should be "put off" until another time, not even for a few minutes. That which ought to be done now should be done now. This seems a little thing, but it is of far-reaching importance. It leads to strength, success, and peace.

The man who is to manifest a cultivated will must also live by certain fixed rules. He must not blindly gratify his passions and impulses, but must school them to obedience. He should live according to principle, and not according to passion. He should decide what he will eat and drink and wear, and what he will not eat and drink and wear; how many meals per day he will have, and at what times he will have them; at what time he will go to bed, and at what time get up. He should make rules for the right government of his conduct in every department of his life, and should religiously adhere to them. To live loosely and indiscriminately, eating and drinking and sensually indulging at the beck and call of appetite and inclination, is to be a mere animal, and not a man with will and reason. The beast in man must be scourged and disciplined and brought into subjection, and this can only be done by training the mind and life on certain fixed rules of right conduct. The saint attains to holiness by not violating his vows, and the man who lives according to good and fixed rules, is strong to accomplish his purpose.

The sixth rule, that of controlling the tongue, must be practised until one has perfect command of his speech, so that he utters nothing in peevishness, anger, irritability, or with evil intent. The man of strong will does not allow his tongue to run thoughtlessly and without check.

All these six rules, if faithfully practised, will lead up to the seventh, which is the most important of them all—namely, rightly controlling the mind. Self-control is the most essential thing in life, yet least understood; but he who patiently practises the rules herein laid down, bringing them into requisition in all his ways and undertakings, will learn, by his own experience and efforts, how to control and train his mind, and to earn thereby the supreme crown of manhood—the crown of a perfectly poised will.

Thoroughness

Thoroughness consists in doing little things as though they were the greatest things in the world. That the little things of life are of primary importance, is a truth not generally understood, and the thought that little things can be neglected, thrown aside, or slurred over, is at the root of that lack of thoroughness which is so common, and which results in imperfect work and unhappy lives.

When one understands that the great things of the world and of life consist of a combination of small things, and that without this aggregation of small things the great things would be nonexistent, then he begins to pay careful attention to those things which he formerly regarded as insignificant. He thus acquires the quality of thoroughness, and becomes a man of usefulness and influence; for the possession or non-possession of this one quality may mean all the difference between a life of peace and power, and one of misery and weakness.

Every employer of labour knows how comparatively rare this quality is—how difficult it is to find men and women who will put thought and energy into their work, and do it completely and satisfactorily. Bad workmanship abounds. Skill and excellence are acquired by few. Thoughtlessness, carelessness, and laziness are such common vices that it should cease to appear strange that, in spite of "social reform," the ranks of the unemployed should continue to swell, for those who scamp their work today will, another day, in the hour of deep necessity, look and ask for work in vain.

The law of "the survival of the fittest" is not based on cruelty, it is based on justice; it is one aspect of that divine equity which everywhere prevails. Vice is "beaten with many stripes"; if it were not so, how could virtue be developed? The thoughtless and lazy cannot take precedence of, or stand equally with, the thoughtful and industrious. A friend of mine tells me that his father gave all his children the following piece of advice:

Whatever your future work may be, put your whole mind upon it and do it thoroughly; you need then have no fear as to your welfare, for there are so many who are careless and negligent that the services of the thorough man are always in demand.

I know those who have, for years, tried almost in vain to secure competent workmanship in spheres which do not require exceptional skill, but which call chiefly for forethought, energy, and conscientious care. They have discharged one after another for negligence, laziness, incompetence, and persistent breaches of duty—not to mention other vices which have no bearing on this subject; yet the vast army of the unemployed continues to cry out against the laws, against society, and against Heaven.

The cause of this common lack of thoroughness is not far to seek; it lies in that thirst for pleasure which not only creates a distaste for steady labour, but renders one incapable of doing the best work, and of properly fulfilling one's duty. A short time ago, a case came under my observation (one of many such), of a poor woman who was given, at her earnest appeal, a responsible and lucrative position. She had been at her post only a few days when she began to talk of the "pleasure trips" she was going to have now she had come to that place. She was discharged at the end of a month for negligence and incompetence.

As two objects cannot occupy the same space at the same time, so the mind that is occupied with pleasure cannot also be concentrated upon the perfect performance of duty. Pleasure has its own place and time, but its consideration should not be allowed to enter the mind during those hours which should be devoted to duty. Those who, while engaged in their worldly task, are continually dwelling upon anticipated pleasures, cannot do otherwise than bungle through their work, or even neglect it when their pleasure seems to be at stake.

Thoroughness is completeness, perfection; it means doing a thing so well that there is nothing left to be desired; it means doing one's work, if not better than anyone else can do it, at least not worse than the best that others do. It means the exercise of much thought, the putting forth of great energy, the persistent application of the mind to its task, the cultivation of patience, perseverance, and a high sense of duty. An ancient teacher said, "If anything has to be done, let a man do it, let him attack it vigorously"; and another teacher said, "Whatsoever thy hand findeth to do, do it with thy might."

He who lacks thoroughness in his worldly duties, will also lack the same quality in spiritual things. He will not improve his character; will be weak and half-hearted in his religion, and will not accomplish any good and useful end. The man who keeps one eye on worldly pleasure and the other on religion, and who thinks he can have the advantage of both conditions, will not be thorough either in his pleasure-seeking or his religion, but will make a sorry business of both. It is better to be a whole-souled worldling than a half-hearted religionist; better to give the entire mind to a lower thing than half of it to a higher.

It is preferable to be thorough, even if it be in a bad or selfish direction, rather than inefficient and squeamish in good directions, for thoroughness leads more rapidly to the development of character and the acquisition of wisdom; it accelerates progress and unfoldment; and while it leads the bad to something better, it spurs the good to higher and ever higher heights of usefulness and power.

Mind-Building
and Life-Building

Everything both in nature and the works of man is produced by a process of building. The rock is built up of atoms; the plant, the animal, and man are built up of cells; a house is built of bricks, and a book is built of letters. A world is composed of a large number of forms, and a city of a large number of houses. The arts, sciences, and institutions of a nation are built up by the efforts of individuals. The history of a nation is the building of its deeds.

The process of building necessitates the alternate process of breaking down. Old forms that have served their purpose are broken up, and the material of which they are composed enters into new combinations. There is reciprocal integration and disintegration. In all compounded bodies, old cells are ceaselessly being broken up, and new cells are formed to take their place. The works of man also require to be continually renewed until they have become old and useless, when they are torn down in order that some better purpose may be served. These two processes of breaking down and building up in Nature are called *death* and *life*; in the artificial works of man they are called *destruction* and *restoration*.

This dual process, which obtains universally in things visible, also obtains universally in things invisible. As a body is built of cells, and a house of bricks, so a man's mind is built of thoughts. The various characters of men are none other than compounds of thoughts of varying combinations. Herein we see the deep truth of the saying, "As a man thinketh in his heart, so is he." Individual characteristics are *fixed processes of thought*; that is, they are fixed in the sense that they have become such an integral part of the character that they can be only altered or removed by a protracted effort of the will, and by much self-discipline. Character is built in the same way as a tree or a house is built—namely, by the ceaseless addition of new material, and that material is *thought*. By the aid of millions of bricks a city is built; by the aid of millions of thoughts a mind, a character, is built. "Rome was not built in a day," and a Buddha, a Plato, or a Shakespeare is not built in a lifetime.

Every man is a mind-builder, whether he recognizes it or not. Every man must perforce think, and every thought is another brick laid down in the edifice of mind. Such "brick-laying" is done loosely and carelessly by a vast number of people, the result being unstable and tottering characters that are ready to go down under the first little gust of trouble or temptation. Some, also, put into the building of their minds large numbers of impure thoughts; these are so many rotten bricks that crumble away as fast as they are put in, leaving always an unfinished and unsightly building, and one which can afford no comfort and no shelter for its possessor. Debilitating thoughts about one's health, enervating thoughts concerning unlawful pleasures, weakening thoughts of failure, and sickly thoughts of self-pity and self-praise are useless bricks with which no substantial mind-temple can be raised.

Pure thoughts, wisely chosen and well placed, are so many durable bricks which will never crumble away, and from which a finished and beautiful building, and one which affords comfort and shelter for its possessor, can be rapidly erected. Bracing thoughts of strength, of confidence, of duty; inspiring thoughts of a large, free, unfettered, and unselfish life, are useful bricks with which a substantial mind-temple can be raised; and the building of such a temple necessitates that old and useless habits of thought be broken down and destroyed.

> *Build thee more stately mansions, O my soul!*
> *As the swift seasons roll.*

Each man is the builder of himself. If he is the occupant of a jerry-built hovel of a mind that lets in the rains of many troubles, and through which blow the keen winds of oft-recurring disappointments, let him get to work to build a more noble mansion which will afford him better protection against those mental elements. Trying to weakly shift the responsibility for his jerry-building on to the devil, or his forefathers, or anything or anybody but himself, will neither add to his comfort, nor help him to build a better habitation.

When he wakes up to a sense of his responsibility, and an approximate estimate of his power, then he will commence to build like a true workman, and will produce a symmetrical and finished character that will endure, and be cherished by posterity, and which, while affording a neverfailing protection for himself, will continue to give shelter to many a struggling one when he has passed away.

The whole visible universe is framed on a few mathematical principles. All the wonderful works of man in the material world have been brought about by the rigid observance of a few underlying principles; and all that there is to the making of a successful, happy, and beautiful life, is the knowledge and application of a few simple, root principles.

If a man is to erect a building that is to resist the fiercest storms, he must build it on a simple, mathematical principle, or law, such as the square or the circle; if he ignores this, his edifice will topple down even before it is finished.

Likewise, if a man is to build up a successful, strong, and exemplary life—a life that will stoutly resist the fiercest storms of adversity and temptation—it must be framed on a few simple, undeviating moral principles.

Four of these principles are—*Justice, Rectitude, Sincerity,* and *Kindness.* These four ethical truths are to the making of a life what the four lines of a square are to the building of a house. If a man ignores them and thinks to obtain success and happiness and peace by injustice, trickery, and selfishness, he is in the position of a builder who imagines he can build a strong and durable habitation while ignoring the relative arrangement of mathematical lines, and he will, in the end, obtain only disappointment and failure.

He may, for a time, make money, which will delude him into believing that injustice and dishonesty pay well; but in reality his life is so weak and unstable that it is ready at any moment to fall; and when a critical period comes, as come it must, his affairs, his reputation, and his riches crumble to ruins, and he is buried in his own desolation.

It is totally impossible for a man to achieve a truly successful and happy life who ignores the four moral principles enumerated, whilst the man who scrupulously observes them in all his dealings can no more fail of success and blessedness than the earth can fail of the light and warmth of the sun so long as it keeps to its lawful orbit; for he is working in harmony with the fundamental laws of the universe; he is building his life on a basis which cannot be altered or overthrown, and, therefore, all that he does will be so strong and durable, and all the parts of his life will be so coherent, harmonious, and firmly knit that it cannot possibly be brought to ruin.

In all the universal forms which are built up by the Great Invisible and unerring Power, it will be found that the observance of mathematical law is carried out with unfailing exactitude down to the most minute detail. The microscope reveals the fact that the Infinitely small is as perfect as the Infinitely great.

A snowflake is as perfect as a star. Likewise, in the erection of a building by man, the strictest attention must be paid to every detail.

A foundation must first be laid, and, although it is to be buried and hidden, it must receive the greatest care, and be made stronger than any other part of the building; then stone upon stone, brick upon brick is carefully laid with the aid of the plumb-line, until at last the building stands complete in its durability, strength, and beauty.

Even so it is with the life of a man. He who would have a life secure and blessed, a life freed from the miseries and failures to which so many fall victims, must carry the practice of the moral principles into every detail of his life, into every momentary duty and trivial transaction. In every little thing he must be thorough and honest, neglecting nothing.

To neglect or misapply any little detail—be he commercial man, agriculturist, professional man, or artisan—is the same as neglecting a stone or a brick in a building, and it will be a source of weakness and trouble.

The majority of those who fail and come to grief do so through neglecting the apparently *insignificant* details.

It is a common error to suppose that little things can be passed by, and that the greater things are more important, and should receive all attention; but a cursory glance at the universe, as well as a little serious reflection on life, will teach the lesson that nothing great can exist which is not made up of small details, and in the composition of which every detail is perfect.

He who adopts the four ethical principles as the law and base of his life, who raises the edifice of character upon them, who in his thoughts and words and actions does not wander from them, whose every duty and every passing transaction is performed in strict accordance with their exactions, such a man, laying down the hidden foundation of integrity of heart securely and strongly, cannot fail to raise up a structure which shall bring him honour; and he is building a temple in which he can repose in peace and blessedness—even the strong and beautiful Temple of his life.

Cultivation of Concentration

oncentration, or the bringing of the mind to a centre and keeping it there, is vitally necessary to the accomplishment of any task. It is the father of *thoroughness* and the mother of *excellence*. As a faculty, it is not an end in itself, but is an aid to all faculties, all work. Not a purpose in itself, it is yet a power which serves all purposes. Like steam in mechanics, it is a dynamic force in the machinery of the mind and the functions of life.

The faculty is a common possession, though in its perfection it is rare—just as *will* and *reason* are common possessions, though a perfectly poised will and a comprehensive reason are rare possessions—and the mystery which some modern mystical writers have thrown around it is entirely superfluous. Every successful man, in whatever direction his success may lie, practises concentration, though he may know nothing about it as a subject of study: every time one becomes absorbed in a book or task, or is rapt in devotion or assiduous in duty, concentration, in a greater or lesser degree, is brought into play.

Many books purporting to give instructions on concentration make its practice and acquisition an end in itself. Than this there is no surer nor swifter way to its destruction. The fixing of the eyes upon the tip of the nose, upon a door-knob, a picture, a mystical symbol, or the portrait of a saint; or the centring of the mind upon the navel, the pineal gland, or some imaginary point in space (I have seen all these methods seriously advised in works on this subject) with the object of acquiring concentration, is like trying to nourish the body by merely moving the jaw as in the act of eating, without taking food. Such methods prevent the end at which they aim. They lead toward dispersion and not concentration; toward weakness and imbecility rather than toward power and intelligence. I have met those who have squandered, by these practices, what measure of concentration they at first possessed, and have become the prey of a weak and wandering mind.

Concentration is an aid to the doing of something; it is not the doing of something in itself. A ladder has no value in and of itself, but only in so far as it enables us to *reach* something which we could not otherwise reach. In like manner, concentration is that which enables the mind to accomplish with ease that which it would be otherwise impossible to accomplish; but of itself it is a dead thing, and not a living accomplishment.

Concentration is so interwoven with the uses of life that it cannot be separated from duty; and he who tries to acquire it *apart from his task, his duty*, will not only fail, but will diminish, and not increase, his mental control and executive capacity, and so render himself less and less fit to succeed in his undertakings.

In the task of the hour is all the means for the cultivation of concentration—whether that task be the acquiring of divine knowledge, or the sweeping of a floor—without resorting to methods which have no practical bearing on life; for what is concentration but the bringing of a well-controlled mind to the doing of that which has to be done?

He who does his work in an aimless, a hurried, or thoughtless manner, and resorts to his artificial "concentration methods"—to his door-knob, his picture, or nasal extremity—in order to gain that which he imagines to be some kind of mystical power—but which is a very ordinary and practical quality—though he may drift toward insanity (and I knew one man who became insane by these practices), he will not increase in steadiness of mind.

The great enemy of concentration—and therefore of all skill and power—is a wavering, wandering, undisciplined mind; and it is in overcoming this that concentration is acquired. A scattered and undisciplined army would be useless. To make it effective in action and swift in victory it must be solidly concentrated and masterfully directed. Scattered and diffused thoughts are weak and worthless. Thoughts marshalled, commanded, and directed upon a given point, are invincible; confusion, doubt, and difficulty give way before their masterly approach. Concentrated thought enters largely into all successes, and informs all victories.

There is no more secret about its acquirement than about any other acquisition, for it is governed by the underlying principle of all development, namely, *practice*. To be able to do a thing, you must begin to *do it*, and keep on doing it until the thing is mastered. This principle prevails universally— in all arts, sciences, trades; in all learning, conduct, religion. To be able to paint, one must paint; to know how to use a tool skillfully, he must use the tool; to become learned, he must learn; to become wise, he must do wise things; and to successfully concentrate his mind, he must concentrate it. But the doing is not all—*it must be done with energy and intelligence.*

The beginning of concentration, then, is to go to your daily task and put your mind on it, bringing all your intelligence and mental energy to a focus upon that which has to be done; and every time the thoughts are found wandering aimlessly away, they should be brought promptly back to the thing in hand. Thus the "centre" upon which you are to bring your mind to a point, is (not your pineal gland or a point in space), but the work which you are doing every day; and your object in thus concentrating is to be able to do your work with smooth rapidity and consummate skill; for until you can thus do your work, you have not gained any degree of control over the mind; you have not acquired the power of concentration.

This powerful focussing of one's thought and energy and will upon the doing of things is difficult at first—as everything worth acquiring is difficult—but daily efforts, strenuously made and patiently followed up, will soon lead to such a measure of self-control as will enable one to bring a strong and penetrating mind to bear upon any work undertaken; a mind that will quickly comprehend all the details of the work, and dispose of them with accuracy and despatch. He will thus, as his concentrative capacity increases, enlarge his usefulness in the scheme of things, and increase his value to the world, thus inviting nobler opportunities, and opening the door to higher duties; he will also experience the joy of a wider and fuller life.

In the process of concentration there are the four following stages:

1. Attention.
2. Contemplation.
3. Abstraction.
4. Activity in Repose.

At first the thoughts are arrested, and the mind is fixed upon the object of concentration, which is the task in hand—this is *attention*. The mind is then roused into vigorous thought concerning the way of proceeding with the task—this is *contemplation*. Protracted contemplation leads to a condition of mind in which the doors of the senses are all closed against the entrance of outside distractions, the thoughts being wrapped in, and solely and intensely centred upon, the work in hand—this is *abstraction*. The mind thus centred in profound cogitation reaches a state in which the maximum of work is accomplished with the minimum of friction—this is *activity in repose*.

Attention is the first stage in all successful work. They who lack it fail in everything. Such are the lazy, the thoughtless, the indifferent and incompetent. When attention is followed by an awakening of the mind to serious thought, then the second stage is reached. To ensure success in all ordinary, worldly undertakings, it is not necessary to go beyond these two stages. They are reached, in a greater or lesser degree, by all that large army of skilled and competent workers which carries out the work of the world in its manifold departments, and only a comparatively small number reach the third stage of *abstraction*; for when abstraction is reached, we have entered the sphere of genius. In the first two stages, the work and the mind are separate, and the work is done more or less laboriously, and with a degree of friction; but in the third stage, a marriage of the work with the mind takes place, there is a fusion, a union, and the two become one: then there is a superior efficiency with less labour and friction. In the perfection of the first two stages, the mind is objectively engaged, and is easily drawn from its centre by external sights and sounds; but when the mind has attained perfection in abstraction, the *subjective* method of working is accomplished, as distinguished from the *objective*. The thinker is then oblivious to the outside world, but is vividly alive in his mental operations. If spoken to, he will not hear; and if plied with more vigorous appeals, he will bring back his mind to outside things as one coming out of a dream; indeed, this abstraction is a kind of waking dream, but its similarity to a dream ends with the subjective state: it does not obtain in the mental operations of that state, in which, instead of the confusion of dreaming, there is perfect order, penetrating insight, and a wide range of comprehension. Whoever attains to perfection in abstraction will manifest genius in the particular work upon which his mind is centred. Inventors, artists, poets, scientists, philosophers, and all men of genius, are men of abstraction. They accomplish subjectively, and with ease, that which the objective workers—men who have not yet attained beyond the second stage in concentration—cannot accomplish with the most strenuous labour.

When the fourth stage—that of *activity in repose*—is attained, then concentration in its perfection is acquired. I am unable to find a single word which will fully express this dual condition of intense activity combined with steadiness, or rest, and have therefore employed the term "activity in repose." The term appears contradictory, but the simple illustration of a spinning top will serve to explain the paradox. When a top spins at the maximum velocity, the friction is reduced to the minimum, and the top assumes that condition of perfect repose which is a sight so beautiful to the eye, and so captivating to the mind, of the schoolboy, who then says his top is "asleep." The top is apparently motionless, but it is the rest, not of inertia, but of intense and perfectly balanced activity. So the mind that has acquired perfect concentration is, when engaged in that intense activity of thought which results in productive work of the highest kind, in a state of quiet poise and calm repose. Externally, there is no apparent activity, no disturbance, and the face of a man who has acquired this power will assume a more or less radiant calmness, and the face will be more sublimely calm when the mind is most intensely engaged in active thought.

Each stage of concentration has its particular power. Thus the first stage, when perfected, leads to usefulness; the second leads to skill, ability, talent; the third leads to originality and genius; while the fourth leads to mastery and power, and makes leaders and teachers of men.

In the development of concentration, also, as in all objects of growth, the following stages embody the preceding ones in their entirety. Thus in contemplation, attention is contained; in abstraction, both attention and contemplation are embodied; and he who has reached the last stage, brings into play, in the act of contemplation, all the four stages.

He who has perfected himself in concentration is able, at any moment, to bring his thoughts to a point upon any matter, and to search into it with the strong light of an active comprehension.

He can both take a thing up and lay it down with equal deliberation. He has learned how to use his thinking faculties to fixed purposes, and guide them toward definite ends. He is an intelligent doer of things, and not a weak wanderer amid chaotic thought.

Decision, energy, alertness, as well as deliberation, judgment, and gravity, accompany the habit of concentration; and that vigorous mental training which its cultivation involves, leads, through ever-increasing usefulness and success in worldly occupations, toward that higher form of concentration called "meditation," in which the mind becomes divinely illumined, and acquires the heavenly knowledge.

Practice of Meditation

When *aspiration* is united to *concentration*, the result is *meditation*. When a man intensely desires to reach and realise a higher, purer, and more radiant life than the merely worldly and pleasure loving life, he engages in *aspiration*; and when he earnestly concentrates his thoughts upon the finding of that life, he practises meditation.

Without intense aspiration, there can be no meditation. Lethargy and indifference are fatal to its practise. The more intense the nature of a man, the more readily will he find meditation, and the more successfully will he practise it. A fiery nature will most rapidly scale the heights of Truth in meditation, when its aspirations have become sufficiently awakened.

Concentration is necessary to worldly success: meditation is necessary to spiritual success. Worldly skill and knowledge are acquired by concentration: spiritual skill and knowledge are acquired by meditation. By concentration a man can scale the highest heights of genius, but he cannot scale the heavenly heights of Truth: to accomplish this, he must meditate. By concentration a man may acquire the wonderful comprehension and vast power of a Caesar; by meditation he may reach the divine wisdom and perfect peace of a Buddha. The perfection of concentration is *power*; the perfection of meditation is *wisdom*. By concentration, men acquire skill in the doing of the things of life—in science, art, trade, etc.,—but by meditation, they acquire skill in *life* itself; in right living, enlightenment, wisdom, etc. Saints, sages, saviours—wise men and divine teachers—are the finished products of holy meditation.

The four stages in concentration are brought into play in meditation; the difference between the two powers being one of *direction*, and not of nature. Meditation is therefore *spiritual concentration*; the bringing of the mind to a focus in its search for the divine knowledge, the divine life;

the intense dwelling, in thought, on Truth. Thus a man aspires to know and realise, above all things else, the Truth; he then gives *attention* to conduct, to life, to self-purification: giving attention to these things, he passes into serious *contemplation* of the facts, problems, and mystery of life: thus contemplating, he comes to love Truth so fully and intensely as to become wholly absorbed in it, the mind is drawn away from its wanderings in a multitude of desires, and, solving one by one the problems of life, realises that profound union with Truth which is the state of *abstraction*; and thus absorbed in Truth, there is that balance and poise of character, that divine *action in repose*, which is the abiding calm and peace of an emancipated and enlightened mind.

Meditation is more difficult to practise than concentration because it involves a much more severe self-discipline than that which obtains in concentration. A man can practise concentration without purifying his heart and life, whereas the process of purification is inseparable from meditation. The object of meditation is divine enlightenment, the attainment of Truth, and is therefore interwoven with practical purity and righteousness. Thus while, at first, the time spent in actual meditation is short—perhaps only half an hour in the early morning—the knowledge gained in that half-hour of vivid aspiration and concentrated thought is embodied in practise during the whole day. In meditation, therefore, the entire life of a man is involved; and as he advances in its practise he becomes more and more fitted to perform the duties of life in the circumstances in which he may be placed, for he becomes stronger, holier, calmer, and wiser.

The principle of meditation is twofold, namely—

1. Purification of the heart by repetitive thought on pure things.
2. Attainment of divine knowledge by embodying such purity in practical life.

Man is a *thought-being*, and his life and character are determined by the thoughts in which he habitually dwells. By practise, association, and habit, thoughts tend to repeat themselves with greater and greater ease and frequency, and so "fix" the character in a given direction by producing that automatic action which is called "habit." By daily dwelling upon pure thoughts, the man of meditation forms the habit of pure and enlightened thinking which leads to pure and enlightened actions and well-performed duties. By the ceaseless repetition of pure thoughts, he at last becomes one

with those thoughts, and is a purified being, man-
ifesting his attainment in pure actions, in a serene
and wise life.

The majority of men live in a series of conflicting desires, passions, emotions, and speculations,
and there are restlessness, uncertainty, and sorrow; but when a man begins to train his mind in
meditation, he gradually gains control over this
inward conflict by bringing his thoughts to a focus
upon a central principle. In this way the old habits
of impure and erroneous thought and action are
broken up, and the new habits of pure and enlightened thought and action are formed; the man
becomes more and more reconciled to Truth, and
there is increasing harmony and insight, a growing perfection and peace.

A powerful and lofty aspiration toward Truth is
always accompanied with a keen sense of the sorrow and brevity and mystery of life, and until this
condition of mind is reached, meditation is impossible. Merely musing, or whiling away the time in
idle dreaming (habits to which the word meditation is frequently applied), are very far removed
from meditation, in the lofty spiritual sense which
we attach to that condition.

It is easy to mistake *reverie* for meditation. This
is a fatal error which must be avoided by one striv-

ing to meditate. The two must not be confounded. Reverie is a loose dreaming into which a man falls; meditation is a strong, purposeful thinking into which a man rises. Reverie is easy and pleasurable; meditation is at first difficult and irksome. Reverie thrives in indolence and luxury; meditation arises from strenuousness and discipline. Reverie is first alluring, then sensuous, and then sensual. Meditation is first forbidding, then profitable, and then peaceful. Reverie is dangerous; it undermines self-control. Meditation is protective; it establishes self-control.

There are certain signs by which one can know whether he is engaging in reverie or meditation. The indications of reverie are:

1. A desire to avoid exertion.
2. A desire to experience the pleasures of dreaming.
3. An increasing distaste for one's worldly duties.
4. A desire to shirk one's worldly responsibilities.
5. Fear of consequences.
6. A wish to get money with as little effort as possible.
7. Lack of self-control.

The indications of meditation are:

1. Increase of both physical and mental energy.
2. A strenuous striving after wisdom.
3. A decrease of irksomeness in the performance of duty.
4. A fixed determination to faithfully fulfil all worldly responsibilities.
5. Freedom from fear.
6. Indifference to riches.
7. Possession of self-control.

There are certain times, places, and conditions in and under which it is impossible to meditate, others wherein it is difficult to meditate, and others wherein meditation is rendered more accessible; and these, which should be known and carefully observed, are as follows:

Times, Places, and Conditions in which Meditation is Impossible.

1. At, or immediately after, meals.
2. In places of pleasure.
3. In crowded places.
4. While walking rapidly.
5. While lying in bed in the morning.
6. While smoking.
7. While lying on a couch or bed for physical or mental relaxation.

Times, Places, and Conditions in which Meditation is Difficult.
  1. At night.
  2. In a luxuriously furnished room.
  3. While sitting on a soft, yielding seat.
  4. While wearing gay clothing.
  5. When in company.
  6. When the body is weary.
  7. If the body is given too much food.

Times, Places, and Conditions in which it is Best to Meditate.
  1. Very early in the morning.
  2. Immediately before meals.
  3. In solitude.
  4. In the open air or in a plainly furnished room.
  5. While sitting on a hard seat.
  6. When the body is strong and vigorous.
  7. When the body is modestly and plainly clothed.

It will be seen by the foregoing instructions that ease, luxury, and indulgence (which induce reverie) render meditation difficult, and when strongly pronounced make it impossible; while strenuousness, discipline, and self-denial (which dispel reverie), make meditation comparatively easy. The body, too, should be neither overfed nor starved; neither in rags nor flauntingly clothed. It

should not be tired, but should be at its highest
point of energy and strength, as the holding of the
mind to a concentrated train of subtle and lofty
thought requires a high degree of both physical
and mental energy.

Aspiration can often best be aroused, and the
mind renewed in meditation, by the mental repetition of a lofty precept, a beautiful sentence or a
verse of poetry. Indeed, the mind that is ready for
meditation will instinctively adopt this practise.
Mere mechanical repetition is worthless, and even
a hindrance. The words repeated must be so appli-
cable to one's own condition that they are dwelt
upon lovingly and with concentrated devotion. In
this way aspiration and concentration harmoni-
ously combine to produce, without undue strain,
the state of meditation.

All the conditions above stated are of the utmost
importance in the early stages of meditation, and
should be carefully noted and duly observed by
all who are striving to acquire the practise; and
those who faithfully follow the instructions, and
who strive and persevere, will not fail to gather in,
in due season, the harvest of purity, wisdom, bliss,
and peace; and will surely eat of the sweet fruits of
holy meditation.

The Power of Purpose

Dispersion is weakness; concentration is power. Destruction is a scattering, preservation a uniting, process. Things are useful and thoughts are powerful in the measure that their parts are strongly and intelligently concentrated. Purpose is highly concentrated thought. All the mental energies are directed to the attainment of an object, and obstacles which intervene between the thinker and the object are, one after another, broken down and overcome. Purpose is the key-stone in the temple of achievement. It binds and holds together in a complete whole that which would otherwise lie scattered and useless. Empty whims, ephemeral fancies, vague desires, and half-hearted resolutions have no place in purpose. In the sustained determination to accomplish there is an invincible power which swallows up all inferior considerations, and marches direct to victory.

All successful men are men of purpose. They hold fast to an idea, a project, a plan, and will not let it go; they cherish it, brood upon it, tend and develop it; and when assailed by difficulties, they refuse to be beguiled into surrender; indeed, the intensity of the purpose increases with the growing magnitude of the obstacles encountered.

The men who have moulded the destinies of humanity have been men mighty of purpose. Like the Roman laying his road, they have followed along a well-defined path, and have refused to swerve aside even when torture and death confronted them. The Great Leaders of the race are the mental road-makers, and mankind follows in the intellectual and spiritual paths which they have carved out and beaten.

Great is the power of purpose. To know how great, let a man study it in the lives of those whose influence has shaped the ends of nations and directed the destinies of the world. In an Alexander, a Caesar, or a Napoleon, we see the power of purpose when it is directed in worldly and personal channels; in a Confucius, a Buddha, or a Christ, we perceive its vaster power when its course is along heavenly and impersonal paths.

Purpose goes with intelligence. There are lesser and greater purposes according with degrees of intelligence. A great mind will always be great of purpose. A weak intelligence will be without purpose. A drifting mind argues a measure of undevelopment.

What can resist an unshakable purpose? What can stand against it or turn it aside? Inert matter yields to a living force, and circumstance succumbs to the power of purpose. Truly, the man of unlawful purpose will, in achieving his ends, destroy himself, but the man of good and lawful purpose cannot fail. It only needs that he daily renew the fire and energy of his fixed resolve, to consummate his object.

The weak man, who grieves because he is misunderstood, will not greatly achieve; the vain man, who steps aside from his resolve in order to please others and gain their approbation, will not highly achieve; the double-minded man, who thinks to compromise his purpose, will fail.

The man of fixed purpose who, whether misunderstandings and foul accusations, or flatteries and fair promises, rain upon him, does not yield a fraction of his resolve, is the man of excellence and achievement; of success, greatness, power.

Hindrances stimulate the man of purpose; difficulties nerve him to renewed exertion; mistakes, losses, pains, do not subdue him; and failures are steps in the ladder of success, for he is ever conscious of the certainty of final achievement.

All things at last yield to the silent, irresistible, all-conquering energy of purpose.

Out of the night that covers me,
    Black as the pit from pole to pole,
I thank whatever gods may be
    For my unconquerable soul.

In the fell clutch of circumstance
    I have not whined nor cried aloud;
Under the bludgeonings of chance
    My head is bloody but unbowed.

It matters not how strait the gate,
    How charged with punishment the scroll;
I am the master of my fate,
    I am the captain of my soul.

The Joy of Accomplishment

Joy is always the accompaniment of a task successfully accomplished. An undertaking completed, or a piece of work done, always brings rest and satisfaction. "When a man has done his duty, he is light-hearted and happy," says Emerson; and no matter how insignificant the task may appear, the doing of it faithfully and with whole-souled energy always results in cheerfulness and peace of mind.

Of all miserable men, the shirker is the most miserable. Thinking to find ease and happiness in avoiding difficult duties and necessary tasks, which require the expenditure of labour and exertion, his mind is always uneasy and disturbed, he becomes burdened with an inward sense of shame, and forfeits manliness and self-respect. "He who will not work according to his faculty, let him perish according to his necessity," says Carlyle; and it is a moral law that the man who avoids duty, and does not work to the full extent of his capacity, does actually perish, first in his character and last in his body and circumstances. Life and action are synonymous, and immediately a man tries to escape exertion, either physical or mental, he has commenced to decay.

On the other hand, the energetic increase in life by the full exercise of their powers, by overcoming difficulties, and by bringing to completion tasks which called for the strenuous use of mind or muscle.

How happy is a child when a school-lesson, long laboured over, is mastered at last! The athlete, who has trained his body through long months or years of discipline and strain, is richly blessed in his increased health and strength; and is met with the rejoicings of his friends when he carries home the prize from the field of contest. After many years of ungrudging toil, the heart of the scholar is gladdened with the advantages and powers which learning bestows. The business man, grappling incessantly with difficulties and drawbacks, is amply repaid in the happy assurance of well-earned success; and the horticulturist, vigorously contending with the stubborn soil, sits down at last to eat of the fruits of his labour.

Every successful accomplishment, even in worldly things, is repaid with its own measure of joy; and in spiritual things, the joy which supervenes upon the perfection of purpose is sure, deep, and abiding. Great is the heartfelt joy (albeit ineffable) when, after innumerable and apparently unsuccessful attempts, some ingrained fault of character is at last cast out to trouble its erstwhile victim and the world no more. The striver after virtue—he who is engaged in the holy task of building up a noble character—tastes, at every step of conquest over self, a joy which does not again leave him, but which becomes an integral part of his spiritual nature.

All life is a struggle; both without and within there are conditions against which man must contend; his very existence is a series of efforts and accomplishments, and his right to remain among men as a useful unit of humanity depends upon the measure of his capacity for wrestling successfully with the elements of nature without, or with the enemies of virtue and truth within.

It is demanded of man that he shall continue to strive after better things, after greater perfection, after higher and still higher achievements; and in accordance with the measure of his obedience to this demand, does the angel of joy wait upon his footsteps and minister unto him; for he who is anxious to learn, eager to know, and who puts forth efforts to accomplish, finds the joy which eternally sings at the heart of the universe. First in little things, then in greater, and then in greater still, must man strive; until at last he is prepared to make the supreme effort, and strive for the accomplishment of Truth, succeeding in which, he will realise the eternal joy.

The price of life is effort; the acme of effort is accomplishment; the reward of accomplishment is joy. Blessed is the man who strives against his own selfishness; he will taste in its fulness the joy of accomplishment.

James Allen:
A Memoir

By Lily L. Allen

from *The Epoch* (February–March 1912)

> *Unto pure devotion*
> *Devote thyself: with perfect meditation*
> *Comes perfect act, and the right-hearted rise—*
> *More certainly because they seek no gain—*
> *Forth from the bands of body, step by step.*
> *To highest seats of bliss.*

James Allen was born in Leicester, England, on November 28th, 1864. His father, at one time a very prosperous manufacturer, was especially fond of "Jim," and before great financial failures overtook him, he would often look at the delicate, refined boy, poring over his books, and would say, "My boy, I'll make a scholar of you."

The Father was a high type of man intellectually, and a great reader, so could appreciate the evident thirst for education and knowledge which he observed in his quiet studious boy.

As a young child he was very delicate and nervous, often suffering untold agony during his school days through the misunderstanding harshness of some of his school teachers, and others with whom he was forced to associate, though he retained always the tenderest memories of others—one or two of his teachers in particular, who no doubt are still living.

He loved to get alone with his books, and many a time he has drawn a vivid picture for me, of the hours he spent with his precious books in his favourite corner by the home fire; his father, whom he dearly loved, in his arm chair opposite also deeply engrossed in his favourite authors. On such evenings he would question his father on some of the profound thoughts that surged through his soul—thoughts he could scarcely form into words—and the father, unable to answer, would gaze at him long over his spectacles, and at last say: "My boy, my boy, you have lived before"—and when the boy eagerly but reverently would suggest an answer to his own question, the father would grow silent and thoughtful, as though he *sensed* the future man and his mission, as he looked at the boy and listened to his words—and many a time he was heard to remark, "Such knowledge comes not in one short life."

There were times when the boy startled those about him into a deep concern for his health, and they would beg him not to *think so much,* and in after years he often smiled when he recalled how his father would say—"Jim, we will have you in the Churchyard soon, if you think so much."

Not that he was by any means unlike other boys where games were concerned. He could play leap-frog and marbles with the best of them, and those who knew him as a man—those who were privi-leged to meet him at "Bryngoleu"—will remember how he could enter into a game with all his heart. Badminton he delighted in during the summer evenings, or whenever he felt he could.

About three years after our marriage, when our little Nora was about eighteen months old, and he about thirty-three, I realized a great change com-ing over him, and knew that he was renouncing everything that most men hold dear that he might find Truth, and lead the weary sin-stricken world to Peace. He at that time commenced the practice of rising early in the morning, at times long before daylight, that he might go out on the hills—like One of old—to commune with God, and meditate on Divine things. I do not claim to have understood him fully in those days. The light in which he lived and moved was far too white for my earth-bound eyes to see, and a *sense of it only* was beginning to dawn upon me. But I knew I dare not stay him or hold him back, though at times my woman's heart cried out to do so, waiting him all my own, and not then understanding his divine mission.

Then came his first book, "From Poverty to Power." This book is considered by many his best book. It has passed into many editions, and tens of thousands have been sold all over the world, both authorized and pirated editions, for perhaps no author's works have been more pirated than those of James Allen.

As a private secretary he worked from 9 a.m. to 6 p.m., and used every moment out of office writing his books. Soon after the publication of "From Poverty to Power" came "All These Things Added," and then "As a Man Thinketh," a book perhaps better known and more widely read than any other from his pen.

About this time, too, the "Light of Reason" was founded and he gave up all his time to the work of editing the Magazine, at the same time carrying on a voluminous correspondence with searchers after Truth all over the world. And ever as the years went by he kept straight on, and never once looked back or swerved from the path of holiness. Oh, it was a blessed thing indeed to be the chosen one to walk by the side of his earthly body, and to watch the glory dawning upon him!

He took a keen interest in many scientific subjects, and always eagerly read the latest discovery in astronomy, and he delighted in geology and botany. Among his favourite books I find Shakespeare, Milton, Emerson, Browning, The Bhagavad-Gita, the Tao-Tea-King of Lao-Tze, the Light of Asia, the Gospel of Buddha, Walt Whitman, Dr. Bucke's Cosmic Consciousness, and the Holy Bible.

He might have written on a wide range of subjects had he chosen to do so, and was often asked for articles on many questions outside his particular work, but he refused to comply, consecrating his whole thought and effort to preach the Gospel of Peace.

When physical suffering overtook him he never once complained, but grandly and patiently bore his pain, hiding it from those around him, and only we who knew and loved him so well, and his kind, tender Doctor, knew how greatly he suffered. And yet he stayed not; still he rose before the dawn to meditate, and commune with God; still he sat at his desk and wrote those words of Light and Life which will ring down through the ages, calling men and women from their sins and sorrows to peace and rest.

Always strong in his complete manhood, though small of stature physically, and as gentle as he was strong, no one ever heard an angry word from those kind lips. Those who served him adored him; those who had business dealings with him trusted and honoured him. Ah! how much my heart prompts me to write of his self-sacrificing life, his tender words, his gentle deeds, his knowledge and his wisdom. But why? Surely there is no need, for do not his books speak in words written by his own hand, and will they not speak to generations yet to come?

About Christmas time I saw the change coming, and understood it not—blind! blind! blind! I could not think it possible that *he* should be taken and *I* left.

But we three—as if we knew—clung closer to each other, and loved one another with a greater love—if that were possible—than ever before. Look at his portrait given with the January "Epoch," and reproduced again in this, and you will see that even then our Beloved, our Teacher and Guide, was letting go his hold on the physical. He was leaving us then, and we didn't know it. Often I had urged him to stop work awhile and rest, but he always gave me the same answer, "My darling, when I stop I must go, don't try to stay my hand."

And so he worked on, until that day, Friday, January 12, 1912, when, about one o'clock he sat down in his chair, and looking at me with a great compassion and yearning in those blessed eyes, he cried out, as he stretched out his arms to me, *"Oh, I have finished, I have finished, I can go no further, I have done."*

Need I say that everything that human aid and human skill could do was done to keep him still with us. Of those last few days I dare scarcely write. How could my pen describe them? And when we knew the end was near, with his dear hands upon my head in blessing, he gave his work and his beloved people into my hands, charging me to bless and help them, until I received the call to give up my stewardship!

"I will help you," he said, "and if I can I shall come to you and be with you often."

Words, blessed words of love and comfort, *for my heart alone* often came from his lips, and a sweet smile ever came over the pale calm face when our little Nora came to kiss him and speak loving words to him, while always the gentle voice breathed the tender words to her—*"My little darling!"*

So calmly, peacefully, quietly, he passed from us at the dawn on Wednesday, January 24, 1912. "Passed from us," did I say? Nay, only the outer garment has passed from our mortal vision. He lives! and when the great grief that tears our hearts at the separation is calmed and stilled, I think that we shall know that he is still with us. We shall again rejoice in his companionship and presence.

When his voice was growing faint and low, I heard him whispering, and leaning down to catch the words I heard—"At last, at last—at home— my wanderings are over"—and then, I heard no more, for my heart was breaking within me, and I felt, for *him* indeed it was "*Home at last!*" but for me—And then, as though he knew my thoughts, he turned and again holding out his hands to me, he said: "I have only one thing more to say to you, my beloved, and that is I love you, and I will be waiting for you; good-bye."

I write this memoir for those who love him, for those who will read it with tender loving hearts, and tearful eyes; for those who will not look critically at the way in which I have tried to tell out of my lonely heart this short story of his life and passing away—for *his* pupils, and, therefore, my friends.

We clothed the mortal remains in *pure white linen*, symbol of his fair, pure life, and so, clasping the photo of the one he loved best upon his bosom—they committed all that remained to the funeral pyre.

About the Author

James Allen was one of the pioneering figures of the self-help movement and modern inspirational thought. A philosophical writer and poet, he is best known for his book *As a Man Thinketh*. Writing about complex subjects such as faith, destiny, love, patience, and religion, he had the unique ability to explain them in a way that is simple and easy to comprehend. He often wrote about cause and effect, as well as overcoming sadness, sorrow and grief.

Allen was born in 1864 in Leicester, England into a working-class family. His father travelled alone to America to find work, but was murdered within days of arriving. With the family now facing economic disaster, Allen, at age 15, was forced to leave school and find work to support them.

During stints as a private secretary and stationer, he found that he could showcase his spiritual and social interests in journalism by writing for the magazine *The Herald of the Golden Age*.

In 1901, when he was 37, Allen published his first book, *From Poverty to Power*. In 1902 he began to publish his own spiritual magazine, *The Light of Reason* (which would be retitled *The Epoch* after his death). Each issue contained announcements, an editorial written by Allen on a different subject each month, and many articles, poems, and quotes written by popular authors of the day and even local, unheard of authors.

His third and most famous book *As a Man Thinketh* was published in 1903. The book's minor popularity enabled him to quit his secretarial work and pursue his writing and editing career full time. He wrote 19 books in all, publishing at least one per year while continuing to publish his magazine, until his death. Allen wrote when he had a message—one that he had lived out in his own life and knew that it was good.

In 1905, Allen organized his magazine subscribers into groups (called "The Brotherhood") that would meet regularly and reported on their meetings each month in the magazine. Allen and his wife, Lily Louisa Oram, whom he had married in 1895, would often travel to these group meetings to give speeches and read articles. Some of Allen's favorite writings, and those he quoted often, include the works of Shakespeare, Milton, Emerson, the Bible, Buddha, Whitman, Trine, and Lao-Tze.

Allen died in 1912 at the age of 47. Following his death, Lily, with the help of their daughter, Nora took over the editing of *The Light of Reason*, now under the name *The Epoch*. Lily continued to publish the magazine until her failing eyesight prevented her from doing so. Lily's life was devoted to spreading the works of her husband until her death at age 84.

CPSIA information can be obtained
at www.ICGtesting.com
Printed in the USA
LVHW022039140221
679287LV00011B/1618